Friday Forward

A 52-Week **JOURNAL**
to Drive You Forward in Your
Goals, Week over Week

ROBERT GLAZER

Published by Simple Truths, an imprint of Sourcebooks.
P.O. Box 4410, Naperville, Illinois 60567-4410
(630) 961-3900
sourcebooks.com

Printed and bound in the United States of America.
SB 10 9 8 7 6 5 4 3 2 1

For everyone who knows deep
down they can be more.

For Chloe, Max, and Zach. You each inspire
me to be better every day.

INTRODUCTION

One of the key principles shared throughout my book *Friday Forward* is the importance of reflection. High achievers are constantly reflecting on what they want most, evaluating their plans or progress toward their goals, and recalibrating their priorities, daily habits, and time commitments as a result. This journal is designed to be a companion to *Friday Forward* and help kick-start that reflection process for you, allowing you to gain some more clarity and start on the path toward building your capacity and reaching your full potential.

I recommend reading, or rereading, a chapter from *Friday Forward* once every week and then answering the corresponding journal prompt. If you do this, you'll find yourself setting the foundation for creating new goals and actionable plans and cultivating the habits and relationships needed to achieve your goals.

This journal is a companion to the hardcover and trade paperback versions of *Friday Forward*, and the chapter titles associated with each journal prompt are assigned accordingly. The journal prompts are listed in the order the chapters appear in *Friday Forward*, regardless of the edition.

HOW TO USE THIS JOURNAL

There's no right or wrong way to answer the prompts in this journal. Make it your own. However, you will get the most value if you push yourself to be vulnerable and introspective in your responses. When a prompt asks you to consider something you wish to improve or to reflect on a weakness you have, don't give the type of response you'd tell an acquaintance or a job interviewer. Push yourself to go deeper.

If it's helpful, here are two example responses that may spark your thinking as you work your way through this journal.

Sample Prompt #1: Having Potential

Prompt: In what facet of life—your relationships, work, health, or other—do you have the most untapped potential? What is one next step you can take to start capitalizing on that potential?

Response: *I've always believed I could be a good public speaker and would love to be paid to speak. I am confident speaking to a room of people, such as making toasts at weddings or giving extended presentations at work, and feel that I make an impact and could do so on a bigger stage.*

What I need to break through is more practice and feedback. I will join my local chapter of Toastmasters, an organization dedicated to helping members practice their speaking skills. I'll attend meetings monthly and watch the videos of my last few presentations at work, which were recorded, to make notes about where I could improve. This should help me reach the point where I am confident enough to try speaking to live audiences, and I will have the practice to back it up.

Sample Prompt # 2: Carpe Diem

Prompt: What is the biggest regret you can imagine having when you look back on your life? What can you start doing now to avoid feeling that regret later?

Response: *While I can imagine living with myself if I fall short of several aspirations, I am genuinely saddened by the possibility of having a distant or strained relationship with my kids. I have seen friends who took their time with their families for* granted, missing important milestones due to work or simply not realizing just how quickly childhood passes. I badly want to avoid this type of regret.

I want to commit to two things now. First, I want to be fully present during my time with my kids—I will give them my full attention when they need help with their homework or want my advice, and I will stop bringing my phone to the table during family dinners. Second, I will make a plan to go on an overnight or weekend trip with each of my kids, separately, each year. I want to be sure each one feels like they are a priority in my life, and I want to build an individual bond with them.

> **I hope you enjoy this journal, and as always, I would love your feedback, which you can send to elevate@robertglazer.com.**

Spiritual
Capacity

Raising Values

"The moral values, ethical codes, and laws that guide our choices in normal times are, if anything, even more important to help us navigate the confusing and disorienting time of a disaster."

—SHERI FINK

What is a value that dictates your daily life? How can you better serve this value in your day-to-day existence?

Scan me with a camera phone for more content!

"One of the scariest things in the world is to stand in front of the mirror and meet yourself."

—PHILIP McKERNAN

Where in your life are you avoiding clarity because you fear the pressure of knowing what you want most?

"Carve your name on hearts, not tombstones. A legacy is etched into the minds of others and the stories they share about you."

—SHANNON L. ALDER

Whose legacy and life principles have had the biggest impact on your own life or character? For what characteristics or accomplishments do you want others to remember you?

Wishing Happiness

"All the happiness there is in this world comes from thinking about others, and all the suffering comes from preoccupation with yourself."

—SHANTIDEVA

What is an experience with a loved one you've been wanting to do but have been delaying? How will you make that a reality, and by what date?

Myth of Work-Life Balance

"There is no such thing as work-life balance. Everything worth fighting for unbalances your life."

—ALAIN de BOTTON

What are some ways you can be more fully present, both in your work and outside of it?

Freedom to Fail

"The greatest successes come from having the freedom to fail."

—MARK ZUCKERBERG

What is something you are avoiding trying because you are afraid to fail? What's the worst that could happen if you fail at it? What is the best that could happen if you succeed?

Man with a Plan

"Success is the best revenge for anything."

—ED SHEERAN

Brainstorm one long-term goal. Then challenge yourself to brainstorm six short-term goals or tasks that will help you build toward that goal, and create deadlines for each.

Long-Term Goal:
Purchase a Beach House in Five Years

Short-Term Goal:
Set aside time to tour your top options

Short-Term Goal:
Find a broker to manage your home search

Short-Term Goal:
Try short rentals in a few towns to determine your favorite location

Short-Term Goal:
Research possible beach towns for your house

Short-Term Goal:
Save $5,000 each year for a down payment

Short-Term Goal:
Determine your budget

Long-Term Goal:

Short-Term Goal:

Short-Term Goal:

Short-Term Goal:

Short-Term Goal:

Short-Term Goal:

Short-Term Goal:

Having Potential

"There is no heavier burden than a great potential."

—CHARLES SCHULZ

In what facet of life—your relationships, work, health, or other—do you have the most untapped potential? What is one next step you can take to start capitalizing on that potential?

A Dad's Influence

"A hundred years from now it will not matter what my bank account was, the sort of house I lived in, or the kind of car I drove. But the world may be different because I was important in the life of a child."

—FOREST E. WITCRAFT

Who is someone in your life who deserves more of your attention, mentorship, or leadership? How can you make a bigger impact on that person's life or career? Consider what you would write to them in a note or letter. Draft it here and think about sending it this week.

Moon Shot

"We choose to go to the moon in this decade and do the other things, not because they are easy, but because they are hard, because that goal will serve to organize and measure the best of our energies and skills."

—PRESIDENT JOHN F. KENNEDY

What is the most audacious goal you can set for yourself? Write it down, and specifically note *why* you want to achieve it and what obstacles you'll need to overcome.

Breaking Bad

"Choosing bad is your only shot at achieving greatness. And resisting it is a recipe for mediocrity."

—FRANCES FREI

List five things in your life you're dedicated to doing with excellence. Then write five things in life that you are willing to be "bad" at in order to prioritize what's most important to you.

Purpose and Pain

"I do believe to my core...that our greatest gifts lie right next to our deepest wounds."

—PHILIP McKERNAN

Reflect on one of the greatest obstacles, challenges, or failures you've faced in life. How did you overcome it? Is there a link you've been overlooking between that experience and what motivates you most in life today?

Carpe Diem

"I have no regrets. I don't think you can afford to."

—ALUN WYN JONES

What is the biggest regret you can imagine having when you look back on your life? What can you start doing now to avoid feeling that regret later?

Scan me with a camera phone for more content!

Intellectual Capacity

Myth of the Overnight Success

"Intelligence without ambition is a bird without wings."

—ANONYMOUS

What is your proudest achievement in life thus far? What were some of the small, conscious steps over many months or years that led you to that achievement?

Sharing Belief

"Sometimes you have to believe in the belief others have in you until your belief kicks in."

—JOHN DIJULIUS

Think of an example of someone who believed in you when you needed it most. Write a thank-you note to that person— either to share with them or keep for yourself as a reminder.

Urgent vs. Important

"What is important is seldom urgent and what is urgent is seldom important."

—UNKNOWN, AS QUOTED BY PRESIDENT DWIGHT D. EISENHOWER

Make the following lists: five things in your life that are Urgent and Important, five things that are Not Urgent and Important, five things that are Urgent and Not Important, and five things that are Not Important and Not Urgent.

You're looking to recreate the Urgent/Important Matrix, an example of which is shown below:

Urgent and Important	**Not Urgent and Important**
Daily crisis management and fire-fighting	Long-term strategic thinking
Daily tasks essential to organizational success	Tasks that advance long-term goals
Plan ahead to keep things out of this box	**Invest time in this area**
Urgent and Not Important	**Not Urgent and Not Important**
Busywork	Time-wasting tasks
To-Dos that don't advance your goals	Unengaging leisure
Delegate or don't prioritize	**Avoid whenever possible**

Urgent and Important	Not Urgent and Important
Urgent and Not Important	**Not Urgent and Not Important**

"If you take care of your mornings, the rest of your life takes care of itself."

—HAL ELROD

A morning routine can make all the difference. See here a side-by-side comparison of a person who has a morning routine and a person who does not:

EMILY'S ROUTINE	STEVE'S ROUTINE
Emily wakes up and settles into her morning routine before turning on her phone, which is located downstairs, far away from her bedroom.	Steve wakes up, grabs his phone off his nightstand, and scrolls through his emails on his phone and social media, seeing all the things he missed from the past night. He also quickly sees work messages about problems that occurred overnight and starts worrying about them.
She meditates silently for ten minutes, then reads *Friday Forward* for ten minutes. Finally, she spends ten minutes writing down things she is grateful for in life.	Steve got distracted by his work emails and is running late for his first meeting. He throws on a pot of coffee and turns on the news in the background as he scarfs down a cereal bar. The negative news stories only agitate him more in his rushed, stressed state.

EMILY'S ROUTINE

Emily then works out for thirty minutes, followed by breakfast and coffee, taking a few minutes to read the paper before she starts work.

She revisits her goals for the quarter and picks the three most important things she can do that day and adds them to her priority list.

Emily sits down to work feeling focused and balanced. She then turns on her phone and begins to answer her emails and start her work as planned. She has a productive few hours before taking a break for lunch.

STEVE'S ROUTINE

Steve sits down to work feeling overwhelmed and in firefighting mode.

Steve had trouble focusing in the morning and doesn't feel fully awake until an hour after he starts working. He skips lunch to make up for lost time.

Brainstorm a fifteen-to-thirty minute morning routine for yourself and write down any steps here. Then, revisit these pages each day next week and follow your routine—and take note of how it makes you feel.

Scan me
with a
camera
phone
for more
content!

Being Lucky

"Shallow men believe in luck... Strong men believe in cause and effect."

—RALPH WALDO EMERSON

Think of an instance in your life or career where you got lucky. What steps did you take before then that, in retrospect, put you in a position to benefit from that luck?

World Class

"Whatever you are, be a good one."

—WILLIAM MAKEPEACE THACKERAY

Write down three important recurring responsibilities—personal or professional. For each one, write down some ideas for how you could fulfill that responsibly at a world-class level. What would giving 100 percent toward each responsibility look like?

Scan me with a camera phone for more content!

Stop-Doing List

"If you want something new, you have to stop doing something old."

—PETER F. DRUCKER

Make your own stop-doing list. What are some bad habits, unproductive routines, or daily tasks you need to stop doing? List five, and write down why you need to stop each one.

Power of Keystone Habits

"If you believe you can change—if you make it a habit—the change becomes real."

—CHARLES DUHIGG

Brainstorm some positive habits you want to build into your life. Pick one, and create a short plan for how you will instill it into your daily life starting this week.

Scan me with a camera phone for more content!

Life Hack

"You can't produce a baby in one month by getting nine women pregnant. It just doesn't work that way."

—WARREN BUFFETT

Select one of Morgan Housel's hacks that you would like to pursue. Write down your commitment to that course and how you will follow through on it.

Scan me
with a
camera
phone
for more
content!

Saying No

"You obligation is to the highest point of contribution you can make."

—GREG McKEOWN

What is something in your life you need to say no to next time you are asked? Write down how you will respond, and save it as a template for future use.

Scan me
with a
camera
phone
for more
content!

BS of Busy

"The cost of a thing is the amount of what I will call life which is required to be exchanged for it, immediately or in the long run."

—HENRY DAVID THOREAU

Reflect on the things you do each day that waste your time— such as busywork that doesn't make you more fulfilled or personal distractions that keep you from focusing on what matters most to you. Write down these time-wasters, and consider how you can remove them from your daily life.

Goals and Standards

"You have competition every day because you set such high standards for yourself that you have to go out every day and live up to that."

—MICHAEL JORDAN

What are some of the non-negotiable standards you live life by? These can be commitments you fulfill at work, how you show up for your family, or things in life you will refuse to do, out of principle. Have you been living up to—or falling short of—any of these standards?

Being Excellent

"How you do anything is how you do everything. Your 'character' or 'nature' just refers to how you handle all the day-to-day things in life, no matter how small."

—DEREK SIVERS

Think of a situation where you know you didn't give your best effort. What was the impact of that subpar effort? What will you do in a similar scenario in the future?

Scan me with a camera phone for more content!

Physical Capacity

Clutch Performers

"When you're one of the leaders of the team, there are no days off."

—TOM BRADY

Think of an important upcoming obligation you have—a speech, a presentation, an athletic competition, etc. How can you deliberately practice more for that event to ensure you are ready for any scenario?

Trough and Peak

"Want to feel wealthy? Take away everything money can buy and look at what you have left."

—SEAN SWARNER

Think about a time a time when you hit a roadblock and thought you could not possibly continue, but did. What helped you to move forward?

The Grind

"The best view comes after the hardest climb."

—ANONYMOUS

Think of a goal that you have found especially difficult to pursue and have been neglecting to focus on lately as a result. Reflect on why you set that goal in the first place, what succeeding will mean for you, and two or three things you can to do push across the finish line.

Breaking Barriers

"I was once a kid in leg braces who could barely put [one] foot in front of the other! Now I have signed a contract with Nike Running!"

—JUSTIN GALLEGOS

Think of someone in your life who you admire for how they overcame a particularly daunting obstacle. How did that person prevail, and what do you admire most about the way they did it?

Character Coach

"We live in a culture that teaches us to promote and advertise ourselves and to master the skills required for success, but that gives little encouragement to humility, sympathy, and honest self-confrontation, which are necessary for building character."

—DAVID BROOKS

Where have you previously let your own standards for character slip in order to get a better outcome for yourself or a loved one? Is there a behavior you have excused or condoned that you now wish you had not? What can you do to avoid a similar situation in the future?

"Individual commitment to a group effort—that is what makes a team work, a company work, a society work, a civilization work."

—VINCE LOMBARDI

Where in your life—family, business, community—can you be a better team member? What do you need to do specifically to fulfill that obligation?

Environmental Effect

"There's just one way to radically change your behavior: radically change your environment."

—BJ FOGG

What are some ways that your environment is getting in the way of your performance? What change can you make to discourage a bad habit and encourage a good one?

True Team Sacrifice

"I am a member of a team, and I rely on the team, I defer to it and sacrifice for it, because the team, not the individual, is the ultimate champion."

—MIA HAMM

Think of an example of a person sacrificing for the greater good that you particularly admire. Why do you find this example so powerful? How can you emulate it in your own life?

"A goal without a plan is just a wish."

—ANONYMOUS

Pick a personal goal of yours where you could benefit from some public accountability. Write down the goal, why you want to achieve it, and a few steps you will take to get there. Then, share this with someone else—a group text with your friends, a Facebook group you are in, or even on social media.

Color War

"The will to win, the desire to succeed, the urge to reach your full potential...these are the keys that will unlock the door to personal excellence."

—ANONYMOUS

What is a something you wish to do at a higher level that requires competing with others? This can either be a milestone you want to hit, a group you want to join, a time you want to beat, or an award you want to win. List two or three ways you could up your game.

Good Sportsmanship

"The key difference between winners and losers is how they win and lose."

—ANONYMOUS

Think of a time in your life where you have been an ungracious winner or a sore loser. What did you learn from those experiences?

"Happiness does not come from doing easy work but from the afterglow of satisfaction that comes after the achievement of a difficult task that demanded our best."

—THEODORE ISAAC RUBIN

Who is a person in your life who can serve as your accountability partner as you pursue your goals? Write down what you want that person to do, and consider how you can approach them to fulfill that role for you. Be sure to offer to do the same for them.

Four Strategies for Working Successfully with an Accountability Partner

1. Ask someone you trust and who cares about your development to serve as your accountability partner.

2. Share some of your long-term goals with your partner, and pick three objectives each week to send to your partner each Monday.

3. Then, each Friday, email your accountability partner, noting if each thing was done or not done.

4. Repeat until you achieve the goals you're pursuing.

Putting Yourself First

"Remember always that you not only have the right to be an individual, you have an obligation to be one."

—ELEANOR ROOSEVELT

What is an area of life where you have stretched yourself too thin recently? What have you not been able to focus on as a result, and what consequences has that inattention caused for yourself and others?

Emotional
Capacity

Energy Vampires

"I have only so much energy in the day and I want to invest it. I want to invest it into the people that I love, the people that are investing back in me."

—DANDAPANI

Make a list of five people you would like to spend more time with and five people you need to give less of your energy to going forward.

PEOPLE TO SPEND MORE TIME WITH	PEOPLE TO SPEND LESS TIME WITH
My spouse/partner	Jeff from Accounting
My children	Next door neighbor who constantly complains
My siblings	My drinking buddies
Friends from my mastermind group	My irresponsible cousin
My workout buddy	My sister in-law

PEOPLE TO SPEND MORE TIME WITH	PEOPLE TO SPEND LESS TIME WITH

With Gratitude

"Gratitude can transform common days into thanksgivings, turn routine jobs into joy, and change ordinary opportunities into blessings."

—WILLIAM ARTHUR WARD

Reflect on what you are grateful for in life and list five examples. Reflect back on those each day over the next week, especially if you find yourself upset or frustrated.

Choice Words

"People evolve, and so your relationships must evolve with them. Care personally; don't put people in boxes and leave them there."

—KIM SCOTT

Think of some difficult feedback you have been withholding from someone in your life. Write down what you want to say, then reread and revise your message to ensure you are happy with your word choice. Then commit to reaching out to that person to set up that conversation.

Scan me with a camera phone for more content!

Love and Hate

"The truth is, human nature is good, not bad."

—RABBI MICHAEL WEISSER

Think of a person in your life who could benefit from some kindness, even if they have not shown you any. Think about how you could extend an olive branch by reaching out to them and offering your support or kindness.

Rose, Thorn, and Bud

"An unexamined life is not worth living."

—SOCRATES

Do the "rose, thorn, bud" exercise for yourself—write down the best part of your day, the worst, and something you are excited about. Then share your responses with a partner, friend, or family member, and ask them to share the same with you.

Having Doubt

"We should be unafraid to doubt. There is no believing without some doubting, and believing is all the more robust for having experienced its doubts."

—JUSTIN HOLCOMB

Write down one or two of your closely held beliefs. Play devil's advocate and openly challenge one of those beliefs. What would it mean if your belief was wrong?

Four Benefits of Travel

"The world is a book and those who do not travel read only one page."

—ANONYMOUS

What is a traveling experience you've had in the past that particularly changed your perspective or taught you valuable lessons? What's a trip you have been wanting to take but have put off?

Random Act of Kindness

"Three things in human life are important. The first is to be kind. The second is to be kind. And the third is to be kind."

—HENRY JAMES

Think of a moment in your life when a stranger showed you kindness. What happened, and how did that experience affect you? How could you do something similar for someone else?

Justifying Our Contradictions

"He that complies against his will is of his own opinion still."

—SAMUEL BUTLER

If you are being honest with yourself, where do you hold two contradictory beliefs (e.g., one may believe the government shouldn't interfere with private businesses but also believe Facebook should be broken up)? Can you also think of a false narrative that you have held onto because you did not want to admit you made a mistake or were wrong?

What Really Matters

"As we express our gratitude, we must never forget that the highest appreciation is not to utter words but to live by them."

—JOHN F. KENNEDY

Where in your life do you think you could be happier if you weren't as focused on being right?

Scan me with a camera phone for more content!

Problem Solving

"The problem is not that there are problems. The problem is expecting otherwise and thinking that having problems is a problem."

—THEODORE ISAAC RUBIN

What is a problem you are facing now that you need to solve? Write it down and list five obstacles you face as part of the problem. Spend the next several minutes brainstorming possible solutions to each of those obstacles.

Embracing Relationships

"Everybody needs somebody."

—MAHALIA JACKSON

Who are one or two people you want to get to know more closely, either in your personal or professional circles? What's a next step you could take to make that happen?

"Our greatest glory is not in never falling but in rising every time we fall."

—OLIVER GOLDSMITH

At some point, you will face an especially arduous week. Write a message to your future self, giving yourself the type of pep talk that will resonate. Then, when that bad week comes, revisit your message.

ABOUT THE AUTHOR

Robert Glazer is the founder and CEO of global partner marketing agency Acceleration Partners.

Under his leadership, Acceleration Partners has received numerous industry and company culture awards, including Glassdoor's Employees' Choice Awards (two years in a row), *Ad Age*'s Best Place to Work, *Entrepreneur*'s Top Company Culture (two years in a row), Great Place to Work and *Fortune*'s Best Small and Medium Workplaces (three years in a row), Digiday's Most Committed to Work-Life Balance, and *Boston Globe*'s Top Workplaces (three years in a row).

Bob is the #1 *Wall Street Journal*, *USA Today*, and international bestselling author of four books: *Elevate*, *How To Thrive in the Virtual Workplace*, *Friday Forward*, and *Performance Partnerships*. He is also the host of the *Elevate Podcast*, a top 20 podcast in entrepreneurship in over twenty countries. Bob is a sought-after speaker by companies and organizations around the world and is a regular columnist for *Forbes, Inc.*, and *Entrepreneur*. He also shares ideas and insights around these topics via Friday Forward, a weekly inspirational newsletter that reaches over two hundred thousand individuals and business leaders across more than sixty countries.

Bob serves on the board of directors for BUILD Boston, is a global leader in Entrepreneur's Organization (EO), and is the founder of The Fifth Night charitable event (fifthnight .org). He is an avid skier, cyclist, reader, traveler, and serial home renovator. You can learn more about Bob at robert glazer.com.

Looking for more?

To get started on your capacity building journey, take the Four Capacities Quiz to see where you can grow most: robertglazer. com/elevate-capacities-quiz/

Try my course on Discovering and Developing Core Values, and start aligning your life to your most important principles: corevaluescourse.com

For resources on each capacity: robertglazer.com /elevate-resources/

For Friday Forwards on Spiritual Capacity: robertglazer .com/category/spiritual-capacity/

For Friday Forwards on Intellectual Capacity: robert glazer.com/category/intellectual-capacity/

For Friday Forwards on Physical Capacity: robertglazer .com/category/physical-capacity/

For Friday Forwards on Emotional Capacity: robertglazer .com/category/emotional-capacity/

To hear interviews with the world's leading CEOs, authors, and thinkers on capacity building, try the *Elevate Podcast*: robertglazer.com/podcast

FRIDAY FORWARD STORIES ONLINE

To find the online versions of the Friday Forward stories featured in this book for sharing and related content, please visit:

fridayfwd.com/stories

JOIN FRIDAY FORWARD

Also, if you haven't yet, sign up to receive Friday Forward each week by going to robertglazer.com/join or by scanning the QR code below.